Basic Wing Chun Kuen Art and Science

by Hendrik Santo

Edited by Robert Chu

Revision 1.1

6 13 3 Publications

$$\vec{F}_{Net} = \frac{\Delta \vec{p}}{\Delta t}$$

Basic Wing Chun Kuen
Art and Science

Dedication

To all internal artists of present and future,

咏春 6.13.3

"I vow that in a future life when I attain Bodhi, my body will be as bright and clear as Vaidurya, flawlessly pure, vastly radiant, majestic with merit and virtue, abiding at ease, adorned with blazing nets brighter than the sun and the moon. Beings dwelling in darkness will be illuminated and will succeed in all their endeavors."

The second vow of the Medicine Buddha

Disclaimer

Please note that the author and publisher of this book are NOT RESPONSIBLE in any manner whatsoever for any injury that may result from practicing the techniques and/or following the instructions given within. Since the physical activities described herein may be too strenuous in nature for some readers to engage in safely, it is essential that a physician be consulted prior to training.

Table of Contents

Editor's Preface

I am delighted to work with my Yik Kam Wing Chun Kuen Sifu, Hendrik Santo, in the release of **Wing Chun Kuen Basic Art and Science**. I first met Hendrik in 1999 following the release of my co-authored work, "Complete Wing Chun: The Definitive Guide to Wing Chun's History and Traditions", when he shared with me the *Yik Kam Kuen Kuit* and the original *Yik Kam Wing Chun Siu Lin Tau* set that he had inherited in his lineage.

As the focus of martial arts has been a major driving force in my life, I was fascinated with an older version of Wing Chun Kuen. I have practiced Wing Chun Kuen for nearly forty years and have written many articles, been the subject of many articles and videos on the subject. As history was one of my interests, I delved into the past and research almost all lineages of Wing Chun.

I learned about Hendrik's life and found that he was a disciple of the great Venerable Master Hsuan Hua in Buddhism, and of different traditions of Qi Gong. We worked on a previous work of **Six Healing Sounds Made Simple**, and now when he wanted to release his other work, I volunteered to edit it.

In this work, you will have experienced Hendrik's more than 40 years of research to improve not only your Wing Chun Kuen, but to also address areas where you can be a balanced human being. Although I have studied other forms of Wing Chun, most have turned out to be unbalanced, preferring to focus as a weapon of self-defense. They have paled in comparison as a holistic art balancing mind, body, and spirit.

Wing Chun Kuen Basic Art and Science will take you on a journey from the Physical Body, addressing the Mind, teach you how to adjust your Breathing, become aware of Energy that courses in your body, explain what is Strength in the martial arts, and how to utilize Momentum, to finally become a holistic and Balanced individual.

As no work is ever completed alone, I want to acknowledge my student, Robert Ting, for his illustrations.

Author's Preface

There are two goals for writing this book:

The first goal is to present what is there in the ancient Chinese internal art as it is in today's language in a comprehensive, scientific, and systematic way. I hope that from here on everyone who studies ancient Chinese internal arts can have a solid, pragmatic, basic view, supported by modern science.

The second goal is to hope that this is a beginning of Wing Chun Kuen to become a part of education offered in formal university as an Asian art study. This is to preserve Chinese culture and to further develop and progress into education which benefits all human beings. The life span of a human life is short; I have spent a big part of my life researching the contents of this book. I hope that what I have done can make a tiny contribution to this field positively to help those who are interested in this field, present and future, and I have completed my duty to all of my teachers in the past.

Finally, I would like to thank *Sifu* Robert Chu, who made this book possible.

Chapter 1

Introduction

If the sky opened up for me,
And the mountain disappeared,
If the seas ran dry, turned to dust
And the sun refused to rise
I would still find my way,
By the light I see in your eyes
The world I know fades away
But you stay

- lyrics from "A Love Before Time"

It is a reality that Ancient technology might not be fully applicable in our era due to the differences of living conditions and evolution. However, the Art and Science behind the Ancient technology will always have value to help others continue the technological evolution.

The objective of this book is to introduce the basics of the ancient Wing Chun Kuen in a simple, comprehensive, and systematic way. Even though this book is written for Wing Chun Kuen; it is applicable to other ancient Chinese internal martial arts, for example, *Tai Ji Quan*, and *Qigong*, *Zhan Zhuang*, Healing arts, and Spiritual meditation; Since these ancient Chinese arts share the same common denominator--- The six core elements, thirteen states, and three system keys.

This book covers the six core elements of the ancient Chinese internal art, the thirteen states within the six core elements, and the three system keys, which serve as a direction for the ancient Chinese internal art.

Six Core Elements, Thirteen states, and Three system keys

An elephant has six body parts: four legs, a head, and a tail. It is of more benefit to separate these different body parts, focus on the details of each part, and then integrate them as a whole, instead of getting lost with the elephant's body and confused between the front legs and the rear legs.

The ancient Chinese internal martial art can be analogous with this elephant metaphor. It also has six parts; that would be the six core elements. The ancient art is not any one of the six core elements but an integration of all six. All six core elements function together at the same time. Every core element is dependent on the other core elements.

The six core elements consist of: Physical body element, Mind element, Breathing element, Energy element, Strength element, and Momentum element. Failing to have a full view on the six core elements and its detail will lead to confusion, a partial or non-functional ancient art. If we were to use the metaphor of the elephant again, we would only have a leg of an elephant.

The thirteen states are the basic states that need to be identified and be handled for the practicing the ancient art. The thirteen states are basic states of the ancient Chinese internal martial art, qigong, healing art, and spiritual meditation practice.

The thirteen states are as the following. There are three states within the physical core element, and they are: the state of open

(1/13), the state of link (2/13), and the state of being light weight (3/13).   There are three states within the mind element, and they are: the state of settled (4/13), the state of being quiet (5/13), and the state of peace (6/13).   There are four states within the breathing element, and they are: the state of breathing with noise (7/13), the state of panting (8/13), the state of chest breathing (9/13), and the state of natural lower abdominal breathing (10/13).   There are three states within the energy element, and they are: the state of readiness (11/13), the state of surfacing (12/13), and the state of Qi handling – this is, Qi using intention (13/13).

By clearly knowing these states, this enables one to be able to identify, develop, and examine one's development or accomplishment in the ancient art effectively; thus, avoiding the never ending speculation or guessing which leads to a waste of effort, or traveling or practicing in an improper direction. Ancient Chinese arts, whether they are a martial art, Qigong, or spiritual meditation, share these thirteen states.

The three system keys are the keys of direction and reality check. They are as the following:

The first key is the key of the reality, that is, the art must be in accord to the law of physics, the human body natural or proper biomechanics, and proper traditional Chinese medicine practice (since it is an Ancient Chinese art); for example, humans are subject to the force of gravity and people can't fly.

The second key is the key of style, which is an art, is bound by its style; for example, Chinese food and Italian food are different styles.

The third key is the keys of variation, that is, there are variations within a style; for example, a T-shirt comes in different sizes and colors.

Furthermore, the sequence of Six Core Elements needs to be in accord with the natural human tendency. That is, one needs to develop the physical element before the mind element; one needs to develop the mind element before the breathing element; one needs to develop the physical element, mind element, and breathing element before one can develop the energy element. Failing to do so will lead to a baseless or unstable development; for example, in order to have a restful mind one needs to have a loose body. A physical body in pain is not likely to support a restful mind.

Also, according to Ancient Chinese art system, the first four core elements --- the Physical Body element, the Mind element, the Breathing element, and the Energy element – is also named as the Body of the art. As an example, the body of the art can be analogous to a car. The last two elements – the Strength element and the Momentum element – are also named as the application of the art. For example, the application of the art can be analogous to the driving techniques of driving a car. Thus, a complete ancient system needs to have both the body of the art and the application of the art, such as the car and driving techniques.

The Golden rules of all Ancient Chinese internal arts practice

Loose in body, quiet in mind, and natural in breathing /movement/ energy flow is the goal and proper direction /handling of all Chinese ancient internal art practice ---- whether they be Qigong, Internal martial arts, healing arts, or spiritual meditation. The instant this golden rule is violated, then the practice is very likely to being a damaging practice to the body, mind, and energy. The bottom line of a proper practice is to take the direction of being loose, quiet, and natural to help the body, mind, breathing, and energy to reset, regain balance, and to strengthen itself, instead of through any manmade manipulation which will cause further imbalance. There is no end in the refinement of loose, quiet, and natural within a proper practice. Thus, an ancient internal art practice is a continuous improvement and refinement journey.

The Ancient Chinese Internal art educational process

Ancient Chinese internal arts education is based on direct experience.   The following steps describe the learning process:

1, the teacher reveals the key points of handling 功理,
2, the teacher shows the process of key points handling practice 功法,
3, the teacher teaches the development process and guides the practice for the student to directly experience the outcome or accomplishment 驗証, and
4, the student continues to refine his or her own accomplishment.

Steps 1 to 3 is named as the "the teacher leads one to enter the door" (師父領進门), and further development relies on individual effort (修行在个人).

It is very different in comparison to today's study, where study is mainly theory speculation or guessing, learning indirectly without a process, with emphasis on mimicking postures, and thinking that everyone is free to interpret the art as one likes. Instead of directly and specifically, as the Ancient method of direct experience, which needs verification, if one has accomplished. Thus, one might spend a life time of guessing and never accomplishing what is needed, or never having entered the door.

Guessing is the biggest time waster. One needs to know what, why, and how, in order to develop effective, efficient skill. Defending and debating when one doesn't know, is another big time waster. So, instead of never-ending defending, take action to find out the facts, and studying it, is the way, instead of getting stuck forever trying to cover up what one doesn't know.

Finally, learning the six core elements can be analogous to installing six sensors in one. With these sensors, one can clearly know the conditions or states of the six core elements to support effective and efficient handling and development.

Chapter 2
Physical body

Get the root: Have no concern for the branch,
Like a Pure Crystal containing a jeweled moon,
When this Wish-Granting Pearl can be understood,
Self-benefit and the benefit of others are forever unending.

- Chan (Zen) patriarch Yung Chia, Tang Dynasty

Physical body is a must for any living being to exist in the physical world. The Physical body can be considered as the platform of a four wheel drive sport utility vehicle. Without the platform, there is no vehicle.

Thus, in any internal arts, be it for martial art, healing, or spiritual practice, the physical body element needs to be developed properly prior to other core elements. In the internal arts, in order for the breathing, energy, strength or force flow to flow smoothly, the physical body must not create blockage, intentionally or unconsciously.

However, It is a fact that due to unconscious habit or injury, a grown human will develop physical blockage. This will cause the other core elements to be stagnated. On one hand, the principles of Traditional Chinese Medicine are based on the flow and amount of energy within one's body. Thus, sickness is caused by blockage of energy flow and or inadequate energy reserve. On the other hand, Ancient Chinese internal martial arts rely on lively strength handling, thus, any blockage or habitual holding in physical body part cause a downgrade in efficiency and effectiveness of other core elements.

Thus, the first practice of Ancient Chinese internal arts is to develop a loose physical body in order to eliminate unnecessary stagnation and blockage in other core elements. Loose or *song* (鬆) in the physical element includes loose in the muscles and joints. Loose means do not create or self-generated counter-productive tension, or use excessive effort to handle the physical body.

However, loose or 鬆 *song* is a clearly defined physical phenomenon which needs to be accomplished or attained, It is not speculation or up for everyone's interpretation.

In order to be able to loose or relax one's body, in general, one has to go through and experience the three states of the physical element. The three states are: 1. Open, 2. Link, and 3. Light.

As written in the Ancient Internal Classic, "In motion, the whole body should be light and agile, with all parts of the body linked as if threaded together." Light and agile is being in the state of lightness. All parts of the body linked is the linked state. To be light is to be based on the linked state, and linked state relies on the open state. One needs to develop it in a step by step sequence.   Unless one has experience in what these states are, it is impossible to speculate what they are with mind.

The development of looseness requires these three states development, in sequence, of the physical element. Otherwise, one will not be able to know what is loose, and not be able to have a stable and repeatable state can be evoked at will.

The following present the process or *Gong Fa* 功法 to get to know, identify, and to develop loose or *song* 鬆。 It is also an open secret that in Ancient Chinese Arts, the process or *Gong Fa* is only passed to the inner circle, because it is the process which is realized or brings the theory into reality. Thus, one can spend a lifetime speculating theory or practice mimicking sets, but one is not able to develop the *gong fu* without the process or *Gong Fa*. Without the *Gong Fa*, one is guessing what is *song* or loose, but one never knows what it is. Thus, one can waste a life time and get nowhere, contrasted with those who were taught the *Gong Fa* can clearly know what it is and are able to develop it within days or weeks, and further refine it in months. To have the *Gong Fa* and thus, able to experience, and identify, and to realize the skill, is called "entering the door" – *Ru Men* 入門。 This is the different between the "indoor student" 入室子弟 and the "non-indoor student" is basically one who never gets to know the *Gong Fa*. Thus, without the *Gong Fa*, there is no solid way to develop the *Gong Fu*. *Gong Fa* will be different from style to style, lineage to lineage, since there are many ways to get to the top of the mountain. Every *Gong Fa* is a process that has its strength sand weaknesses. In the evolution of a style or lineage, it is common that a better or more effective, efficient *Gong Fa* is developed. There are also situations in which the entire *Gong Fa* process is not transmitted or lost which completely terminates the lineage or style.

The following is an example of basic *Gong Fa* or process for experiencing and identifying the Loose Body.

AWARE

In order to loosen the physical body, one needs to aware of every part of the physical body from toe to head. The following is an exercise to aware of one's physical body.   First lie down with the back well supported on a firm bed or flat surface that is comfortable. Make sure that the neck and head is well supported by a pillow.

Play with each part by of the body by slowly rotating to the left and right, from feet up to the head. The sequence is as following: feet, ankle, knees, hips, shoulder blades, shoulders, elbow, wrists, fingers, and neck. While playing with each part of the physical body, one pays attention and observes that particular part of the body only. Spend a few minutes playing, getting to know, and familiarizing yourself with each particular part of the physical body.

Awareness and observing different parts of the body is a very important practice. It is similar to the installation of a sensor for monitoring the body element. Often, one thinks one knows one physical body, however in reality, one's mind doesn't have any idea on the physical body until one is aware and observes with the particular part of the physical body to gain a direct experience of that particular part of the body. Furthermore, being aware and observing of the Six Core Elements and Thirteen States transforms one, similar to installing six sensors into oneself. These will right away cause one to live in a very different paradigm, where one suddenly has direct access and gains control of or handles the body mind energy in a short period of time. Once that happens, one will no longer return to the past where all the "sensors" have not been installed and one is caught in the trap of guessing.

Open

Open means to let every part of the physical body unwrap itself naturally. The following is an exercise for experience the opening up or "unwrapping" the body parts.

After completing the above Aware Exercise, continue with lying down comfortably and quietly on the bed, and stay in the position for 5-10 minutes without moving any parts of your body. Let all joints and muscles relax and "unwrap" themselves. Observe how the body unwraps by itself and identify this state of this unwrapping, or opening up, this is the Open State.

Link

The State of Linking is possible only after one is able to let the physical body unwrap or open itself as in the above observation or exercise.

Continue with Open Exercise, while in a state of being open, one slowly, gradually, smoothly, and lightly starts to move the feet or different the joints similar to the Awareness Exercise; moving one part at a time without using excessive force. The body stays within the Open State while moving the observation part of the body. One observes and identifies how the body moves in a slow, gradual, loose and smooth way. This is the experience of the Linked State.

Light

The Light State is a further development, or an advanced state, of the Linked State, where the body can be moved in an open and linked way, effortlessly. The following Ancient Classic is the description of the light state, "A feather cannot be placed, and a fly cannot alight on any part of the body. The opponent does not know me; I alone know him." The Light State is the basis of listening to *Jin* (force flow). Unless one has accomplished this state, listening is not likely because one's physical body is still at the inefficient state which might be caused by unnecessary holding or tensing.

Notice that the above exercises are all done while laying down when the body is at rest. This is why we use the laying down position to minimize unnecessary tension, stress, unconscious holding, or withstanding of the body, while observing the different states.

In addition, the experience in the States identified from the above observation exercises are a baseline reference one can used to compare with one's practice of the art. Since the laying down position is the easiest position compared to the Standing position.

After one has observed the open, link, and light state while laying down, one can further observe the Three States with a natural standing up position such as in *Zhan Zhuang*.

One can further compare the Three States accomplishment in standing, with the experience of the Three States while lying down experience as a reference. One can continue to fine tune the Open, Linked, and Light State while standing, using the lying down experience as a reference.

The above are the basic keys of being aware, observing, identifying, and experiencing the Loose State in the physical body, under static and dynamic conditions, instead of blindly using brute force in the physical body.

Stretching comes after the development of looseness. Without good experience or development in looseness, one will often default to brute force stretching which is likely to create injury or damage. Stretching training needs to be carried out with caution because certain stretching might cause problems for people with illness such as high blood pressure.

A drill such as the repeat practicing of a set without knowing the *Gong Fa* process is named as *Zhao* 操 ; whereas practice of the set with the *Gong Fa* process is to refine one's skill, is named as *Gong* 功. Thus, there is a difference between these practices. The ancient writing or *Kuen Kuit* of a set usually describes the proper practice, or process needed to be follow while practicing a set to develop the *gung fu*; The following is an example of *Kuen Kuit* for the Yik Kam Wing Chun lineage *Siu Lin Tau* set:

Y7 神寄指爪袖底旁。
Pay attention to the finger, claw, and the side under the sleeve.

Y8 旋迴自然順脈氣
Spiral twisting naturally, follow the breathing and the direction of the Qi channel.

Y9 掌背向外神意足。
Back of Palm Faces Outward, Intention and *Shen* needed to be present fully.

Y10 翻掌抽纏對心防
Rotating palm reeling to guard the heart.

Y11 單橫相撐合氣運。
Single horizontal and double press needs to be handled according to inhaling and exhaling.

Internal art and external art

Internal art and external art can be defined as the following:

Loose (light state), tough, continuous and gradual, means "Soft" or *Rou* 柔. Loose (light state), tough, sharp, and speedy means "Hard" or *Gang* 剛. These are within the internal arts domain.

Tense, rigid, and brute force is an external art.

In addition, a proper and well developed Physical body element and movement for the internal art is an upward/ downward, left/right, and inner body/outside body fully synchronized movement. As is stated in the Ancient Classic, "In motion, the whole body should be light and agile, with all parts of the body linked as if threaded together. The energy supporting the physical should be free flowing; the energy supporting the mind activity should be internally gathered. The postures should be without defect, without hollows or projections from the proper alignment; in motion, the Form should be continuous, without stops and starts."

It is impossible for one to develop the internal arts be it martial arts, Qigong, or healing arts when the lower part of the body is tensed or held up, and mimics dance-like loose or soft with arm and upper body. That is because the Physical Body Element is the mother or platform of all other core elements. Without attaining the open, linked, and light states, there is no base to further develop the other core elements. This is a reality all practitioners of Ancient Chinese Arts have to face.

Chapter 3

Mind

Purify the five eyes; attain the five powers,
Simply accomplish them and know what's hard to fathom,
Shapes in a mirror are not hard to see,
But, how can one pluck out the moon in the water?

Zen Patriarch Yung Chia, Tang Dynasty

In today's world, in the context of the Chinese Ancient arts, "Mind" is a confusing term. It can range from religious belief, to wishful thinking, to Zen philosophy, to anything new age spiritual ones like to claim as "Awakened", or "Enlightened", or "Realized". However, a common result of these claims is that none can deliver when it comes to Ancient Chinese Arts, all they can do is speculate. The Mind Element is very specific in the Ancient Chinese Arts. In fact, it is similar to one's own hand - where one knows and is able to use it at will. Never is it a philosophy or clever debate, as in the past, "Head to Mouth Zen".

Loose in the Mind Element means to release mental pressure, that is, to stay in a peaceful state.

Loose in Physical Element and Loose in the Mind Element are mutual supporting. Being physically loose leads to ease of mind. Being mentally loose leads to being further physically loose.

Mind will not function well under a stressful mental state. Physical movement also will be clumsy and slow.

While in a silent or quiet state of mind, the physical body will be sensitive and agile, while at the same time blood circulation is also improved. These make the handling of the body more effective.

Mind Element is similar to the control system computer of a four wheel drive sport utility vehicle. Unless we know the different applications software installed within the computer, we can't get ahold of it, we don't know how, and we cannot use it.

Mind element has four functions, namely those of: Thinking, Intention, Visualization, and Awareness.

Thinking – This is the process of using your mind to consider something carefully.   For example, doing the calculation of 656 x 45 in the mind.

Intention – Intention is giving direction, such as pressing a door bell.

Visualization – To form mental images or pictures in one's mind, such as picturing the trajectory of a cannon ball.

Awareness – is consciousness at the present moment, no thinking, no intention, no visualization.

By knowing these four functions, one can then switch to different function to serve different needs, instead of trapping in the thinking function, and unaware of there is much more than thinking.

In Zen, the "Unfettered mind", or "Immovable mind", *Bu Dong Xin* 不動心 are mentioned; In internal arts or Qigong Classics, Silence or *Jing* 静 is mentioned. These all are based on the stability of the mind element.

There are three Stable States within the Mind Element which needs to be developed for martial arts practice, Zen, qigong, or healing arts. They are namely, the State of Settle(d), the State of Quiet, and the State of Peace. Unless one develops these States, one really cannot handle much under pressure. These Three States are a common denominator of the Daoist, Buddhist, and Confucius' teachings and practice. The following is the description from Confucius teaching to clarify these states.

The States of Settle(d), Quiet, and Peace comes from the Confucius teaching, "The Great Learning" (大学). It says, "Knowing what thoughts to stop, one then accomplishes to the settle(d) down state of mind, after settle(d) down the mind, one is able to accomplish quiet in mind, and after, one proceeds to accomplish peace " (知止而后有定，定而后能靜，靜而后能安). These Three States are also parallel with Daoist or Buddhist mind cultivation practice. It is the common denominator of all mind stability practices.

"Knowing what thoughts to stop" (知止), can be illustrated when one does not continue on, the thoughts suddenly stop spontaneously.

"One then accomplishes the settle(d) state of mind" (而后有定), can be illustrated as after one does not continue on spontaneous thoughts arising within the mind, then one can settle down to doing without other thoughts.

"After one settles down the mind, one is able to accomplish quiet in mind" (定而后能靜), can be illustrated as, after one mindfully drives a car, one does not give rise or pay attention to spontaneous thoughts. The mind is then at a quiet state of mindfulness with low noise or absent of spontaneous thoughts.

"Proceeding to after quiet in mind, one then accomplishes a peaceful state of mind" (靜而后能安), can be illustrated as after one resides at the quiet mindfulness state, one further accomplishes to not be bothered by the external chaos, or worry within the mind.

In practicing internal arts, be it qigong, meditation, or internal martial arts, one must enter into the Settle(d) State in order to start practice. To be effective in making best use of the body mind and energy for internal practice, one needs to be in the Quiet State. To be able to proceed further, one needs to be able to enter into Peaceful State at will; it is at the Peaceful State one is able to deal with stress, worries, fear, and pressure thoughts or external circumstances.

Unless one attains the Settle(d) State, one can't effectively start the internal practice. Unless one attains the Quiet State, one cannot achieve a highly effective and efficient internal art practice. Unless one attains the Peaceful State, one cannot effectively deal with internal fearful thoughts or external pressure.

In Ancient China, a simple technique for develop these states is the recitation of "*Amitoufo*" name. This is simply the chanting of the *Amitaba* Buddha's name in Chinese pronunciation practice. By practicing this recitation, one will enter into the Settle(d), Quiet, and Peaceful States directly, proportional to the effort one spends on practice.

The following is the method of this reciting *Amitoufo* practice, also known as the Buddha-recitation Samadhi practice:

> Sit comfortably with ease with the Physical Body Element in the Loose State. Recite "*Amitoufo*" with one's heart/mind and mouth. The mouth moves slightly, the tongue moves, but one is not making any sounds. Slowly, at the same time, use the ears to listen to the "no sound" sound of the "*Amitoufo*" recitation from the mouth. Make sure recitation is with ease, is effortless, and not too fast. Any strain, stress, pressure feeling in the chest or throat, is an indication of

one must cut down the effort or turn down the recitation speed, until one recites comfortably or effortlessly.

The theory of this reciting *Amitoufo* practice is documented in the *Shurangama Sutra*:

"I remember when, as many aeons ago as there are sands in the Ganges, a Buddha called Limitless Light appeared in the world. In that same aeon there were twelve successive Thus Come Ones; the last was called Light Surpassing the Sun and Moon. That Buddha taught me the Buddha-recitation *Samadhi*...."

The Buddha was asked about perfect penetration. "I would select none other than gathering in the six organs through continuous pure mindfulness to obtain *samadhi*. This is the foremost method."

In addition, what is called "Spirit" or *Shen* 神 in Chinese, also belongs to the Mind Element. The term *Shen* is a confusing term in this era, which can be translated as "God", "Magical", and other vague terms.

As in the 1840 Red Boat era *Siu Lin Tau* writing, "Focus the intention, union with the *Shen*, standing in the equal shoulder stance" (聚意會神平肩檔).   In the *Emei 12 Zhuang* writings, "Intention is in action, *Shen* is right there" (意動神到). In the *Taiji* classics writing, "The *Shen* should be internally gathered" (神宜內斂). *Shen* is simply the energy which supports the mental or mind function. When this energy is drained, or weakened, or deficient, one will be in a dull or absent-minded or forgetful state. For example, imagine how you feel after three sleepless nights, or after a long stressful meeting, or long hours working with computers. When one takes a cup of coffee, or a can of a caffeinated drink, to try to boost one's mental ability, that is an indication that the *Shen* has become weak. In fact, even after taking a caffeine drink or other stimulant, will cause the mind to be dull when the physical body is tired and the

Shen is deficient. Long term using chemicals to boost the *Shen* causes the draining of body energy and imbalance.

An important key in the internal practice is as the internal classics say, "The *Shen* should be internally gathered" (神宜內斂). This means one should not be staring hard with eyes. Staring is draining the *Shen* externally, it is opposite to internal gathering the *Shen*. Furthermore, eyes are directly connected to the Liver Qi. Staring will cause an excited Liver Qi, cause eye strain, or even dizziness.

After learning the Four Functions of the Mind, the Stability of Mind, and the *Shen* or energy which support the mental activity in the mind element, one can actually observe one's mind function, mind stability, and *Shen* at every instant in one's daily life. This is akin to installing a sensor in oneself to be able to detect and handle oneself more effectively and more efficiently. Mind is similar to the hands, only when one knows what it is, one can monitor it, get ahold of it, make use of it, and improve its handling.

"Wisdom" is another term within the mind element. "Wisdom" is also a very confusing term. Wisdom is defined as an ability to see things clearly with a stable mind and not be trapped in, or attached to one's own thinking, or external phenomenon. And "trapped in or being attached to", means that one is lost in one's own mind. For example, after one sits in the cinema to watch movie for ten minutes, one is influenced by the movie to laugh or cry, unaware that it's a just a movie.

Wisdom is never something magical, or a nice philosophy, or fortune telling, or short cuts in detailed thinking. Even if the Buddha, with all his wisdom, lived in our era, he would also have to learn to drive a car, if he needed. The only different between the Buddha and us ordinary people is, it might take the Buddha to learn it in twenty minutes due to his accomplishment in the Mind Element, while we would need twenty hours to learn.

Chapter 4

Breathing

There is only breathing and Qi,
Stillness is developed from the active,
the intention shifts and the Shen is right there.

---- *Emei 12 Zhuang*

Breathing is the bridge between body and mind.

There are four states of breathing one should know in order to be able to handle the breathing properly. The four states of the breathing elements are:

The first state is the **Breathing with Sound State**. The breathing is forceful, crude and audible. One can experience and identify this state by doing jumping jacks for a few minutes until out of breath. One feels short of breath, breathing is rapid and shallow, accompanied with an audible sound.

The second state is the **Panting State**. Breathing in this State feels forceful, stuck, stagnated, and not smooth. One can experience and identify this state by purposely extending the inhale and exhale to the point it is uncomfortable in the chest.

The third state is the **Shallow Chest Breathing State**. In this state, breathing is the common shallow chest breathing. Here, one can experience and identify this state by observing one's daily breathing.

The fourth state is the **Full Body Breathing**. In this State, the breathing is the natural lower abdominal effortless breathing. One can experience and identify this state by lying down comfortably, as in the Physical Body Element Open State; and then observing one's breathing by paying attention to the lower abdomen and hip areas above the genitals, and the area between perineum. With this observation, one will experience the natural lower abdominal effortless breathing and observe how the lower abdomen, hip, and genital areas expand and contracting light, freely, and naturally.

For proper ancient internal art practice, Breathing with Sound places the body in an improper and chaotic state. One must avoid this state to prevent health problems.

Breathing in a Panting state causes Qi flow stagnation. This is also an improper breathing state, and one must avoid this state to prevent create health problems.

The Normal Chest Breathing State is ordinary breathing for common people.

Effortless Natural Lower Abdominal Breathing State is a beneficial state the Ancient Internal Arts practitioners stay in. This type of Natural Lower Abdominal Breathing, in general, has a three to six times larger breathing volume compared with the Normal Chest Breathing State.

With the above four states in the breathing element identified, this can be analogous to one installing a breathing sensor in the body, which makes it possible to monitor and handle one's breathing in daily living.

Furthermore, the Ancient Chinese Internal Arts used these different types of lower abdominal breathing practice. Compared with ordinary shallow chest breathing, these lower abdominal breathing practices have a characteristic of having lower breathing frequency, or lower per minute breathing repetition, and larger breathing volume or amplitude.

Natural Lower Abdominal Breathing is the type of breathing where the lower abdomen expands at inhale. Reverse breathing, or reverse lower abdominal breathing, is the type of breathing where the lower abdomen contracts at exhale. Reverse lower abdominal breathing is in general use for martial art conditioning, while natural lower abdominal breathing is for tuning, balancing, and growing energy. Thus, the natural lower abdominal breathing is also used for healing qigong. Or it may be used as a compliment in martial art practice, after the reverse lower abdominal breathing.

When needed, one pays attention to the exhale phase, and allow the inhale to be natural. However, one must not overstretch the exhale to cause imbalance with the breathing, as that will cause body and mind disruption.

With a proper breathing practice the breathing repetitions per minute (rpm) will decrease naturally after some time of practice. It is common for a practitioner starting with a breathing repetition of 16 repetitions per minute drop to 8 rpm. After a long term of practice, the breathing may drop down to as low as 4 rpm. As breathing effectiveness and efficiency increases, and becomes less dissipative, it will provide health benefit.

Under the same inhale volume per minute, the lower per minute repetition breathing has a higher volume of fresh air intake, when compared to the higher repetition per minute breathing.

Using an example of 12 repetitions per minute breathing, with 150 mL rpm as residue from the previous exhale, and breathing volume at 500 mL:

Breathing volume per minute = 12 x 500 = 6000 mL per minute

Effective fresh air breathing volume per minute = 12 x (500 − 150) = 4200 mL per minute

When compared to 24 repetitions per minute breathing, with 150 mL rpm as residue from a previous exhale, and breathing volume at 250 mL:

The breathing volume is 250 mL breathing volume per minute = 24 x 250 = 6000 mL per minute

Effective fresh air breathing volume per minute = 24 x (250 – 150) = 2400 mL per minute

From the example above, the fresh air intake of 12 rpm breathing has a volume of 4200 mL fresh air per minute, whereas 24 rpm breathing has a volume of 2400 mL fresh air per minute, which is significantly lower compared with 12 rpm breathing.

General rules for breathing and physical movement coordination are as the following:

Inhale at rising and exhale at sinking. Inhale at expanding and exhale at contracting. Inhale at pulling back and exhale at extending. Inhale at storing and exhale at issuing. Inhale at upward movement and exhale at downward movement.

The following are guidelines for breathing practice:

1. Practice when one is with comfortable mind and body state. Avoid practice under mental or physical tired condition.
2. Practice in a place with fresh air. Avoid a polluted area.
3. Do not inhale with mouth.
4. Avoid rapid breathing and long period of coarse and forceful prolonged breathing.
5. Do not practice when hungry or right after a meal. Drink a cup of warm water or milk before practice, if one is hungry. Practice an hour after a meal. Eat a meal 30 minutes after practice.

Finally, regardless if it is Natural Lower Abdominal Breathing, or Reverse Lower Abdominal Breathing, the breathing is required to be quiet, natural, and not forceful during the length of breathing. Breathing needs to be fine, even, soft, and gradual. One should never breathe forcefully or with effort. These are to satisfy the needs of both martial arts and health development.

Chapter 5
Energy

The whole body must be effortless.
Follow the natural flow of breathing and Qi channels.
Taste the details is the wonderful instruction.

---- *Emei 12 Zhuang*

The Yellow Emperor's Inner Canon, or *Huang Di Nei Jing* 黃帝內經 is an Ancient Chinese medical text that has been treated as the fundamental doctrinal source for Chinese Medicine for more than two millennia. This is the root of the Qi, or energy theory, and practice for Chinese Medicine, Internal Martial Arts, Qigong, and healing arts.

Qi means *energy* in today's language. There are many different types of Qi or energy in Ancient Chinese arts. Today, Qi can be viewed as bio-chemical energy, bio-electrical energy, bio-thermal energy or the energy behind multiple processes within the body. It is more important to know what it is, rather than to debate who is right, as many have done. Science and technology are continually improving in human evolution, and thus, the Ancient Science might not be completely correct and accurate. *The Ancients spoke metaphorically.* The modern science might not be advanced enough, at this point, to explain what is behind the ancient practices. Thus, it is much more beneficial to study what it is, as it is, and to see how things worked for the Ancients. The point is to know what the *Qi*/Energy is, and to be able to repeat what works, and to avoid what is known to cause damage, instead of debating or arguing with speculation.

For the Ancient Chinese, the term *Qi* refers to different things under different specifics. Qi refers to breathing within the Breathing Element; Qi refers to the force vector path within the Force Flow Element; Qi refers to the physical object trajectory within the Momentum Element, and Qi refers to energy within the Qi Element. In addition, the function of Qi when it is working with the force flow or *Jin* 劲, can be viewed as a lubricant, which supports the mechanics of force flow handling, instead of some kind of supernatural power.

Since Ancient Internal arts, be they martial arts, healing arts, or qigong follow the traditional Chinese Medicine theory and practice, it is a must to know the channel system in Traditional Chinese Medicine. (*Editor's note: Many referred to the Channel System as a "channel" system, which would be viewed as 2 dimensional. The modern trend in Chinese Medicine is to call it the "Channel" system, denoting it is three dimensional.*) It is recorded in many Ancient martial arts documents that one is required to know the Qi channel system in order to have a proper understanding and practice of the internal arts. Examples of these documents are as the following:

1. The Internal *Gong* scripture of *Xing Yi Quan*, the *Nei Gong Si Jing* 内功四经, which states clearly that it is a requirement to know the Qi channel system for proper practice;

2. The *Emei 12 Zhuang* 峨嵋十二庄 scripture is based on the Qi channel system; and

3. The 1840 Red boat era *Yik Kam Wing Chun Kuen Siu Lin Tau* 易金系小練頭歌诀 instruction requires one to follow the Qi channel system.

Channel System in Traditional Chinese Medicine

A channel is an energy flow in the human body. Qi or energy flows through this channel throughout the body. The channel describes the overall energy distribution system of TCM; describing how Qi, blood, and body fluids of the body permeate the whole body.

The individual channels themselves are carrying, holding, or transporting qi, blood and body fluids throughout the body. Channels flow within the body and not on the surface. They exist in corresponding yin and yang pairs and each channel consists of many acupuncture points along its path to have access to.

The channel system of the human body is an intricate web of interconnecting energy channels. A brief understanding of the channel system will help one to understand the flow of Qi in the body.

There are twelve main channels throughout the body with Qi. Each limb is traversed by six channels, three Yin channels on the inside, and three Yang channels on the outside. Each of the twelve regular channels corresponds to the five Yin organs (Liver, Heart, Spleen, Lungs, and Kidney) and the Pericardium, and the six Yang organs (Gall Bladder, Small Intestine, Stomach, Large Intestine, Urinary Bladder, and *San Jiao*). These are organs that have a relationship to the anatomical counterpart in Western medicine, but in Chinese Medicine, we are more concerned with the relationship to key processes in the body. It is also important to remember that organs should not be thought of as being identical with the physical, anatomical organs of the body, although there is a relationship.

Qi flows in a precise manner through the twelve regular channels as in the following sequence:

First, Qi flows from the chest area along the three arm Yin channels (Lung, Pericardium, and Heart) to the hands. There they connect with the three paired arm Yang channels (Large Intestine, *San Jiao*, and Small Intestine) and flow upward to the head.

In the head, they connect with their three corresponding leg Yang Channels (Stomach, Gall Bladder and Urinary Bladder) and flow down the body to the feet.

In the feet, they connect with their corresponding leg Yin channels (Spleen, Liver, Kidney) and flow up again to the chest to complete the cycle of Qi.

A summary of the above qi flow sequence is also name as Yin rising (where the qi flows up to the chest along the leg yin channel), and Yang sinking (where qi flows down to the feet along the leg yang channel).

Editor's note: For those of you unfamiliar with the Classical Chinese Medicine Channel system, we have included a brief summary and detailed charts to show you the flow of Qi in the channels in the next few pages.

Ren Channel – The *Ren* Chanel is on the anterior centerline. It is responsible as the Sea of Yin and all Yin Channels flow into it. Ren Channel is thought to govern reproduction.

Ren Channel

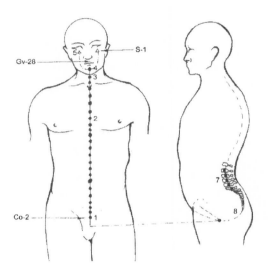

Du Channel – The *Du* Channel is along the posterior centerline. It is responsible for governing the Yang channels in the body, and all the Yang Channels flow into the Du Channel. Du Channel regulates the brain.

Du Channel

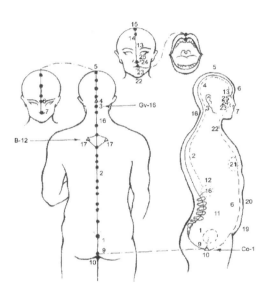

Lung Channel – The Lungs control respiration, and disperses into the skin and hair.

Lung Channel

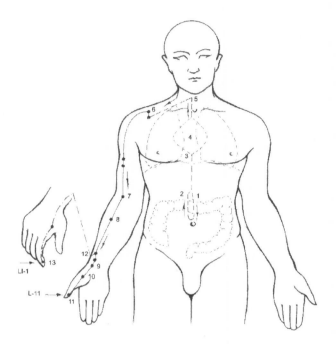

Large Intestine Channel – The Large Intestine receives waste and absorbs water

Large Intestine Channel

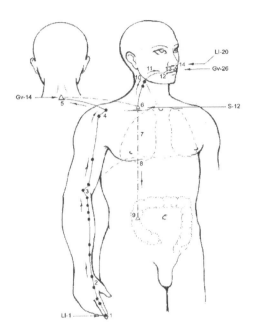

Stomach Channel – Receives and "decomposes" food

Stomach Channel

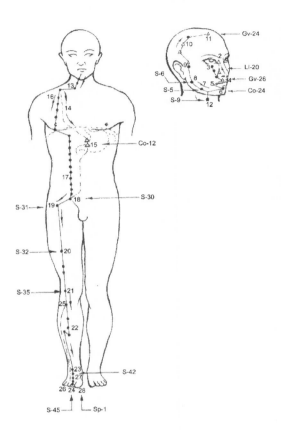

Spleen Channel – Transforms and transports food into blood and energy, controls the flow of blood in vessels, and dominates the muscles and functions of the four limbs, opens into the mouth, and manifests in the lips.

Spleen Channel

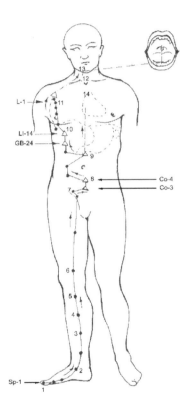

Heart Channel - The Heart is referred to as the "Emperor", and dominates blood and vessels, houses the *Shen* (Spirit), and opens into the tongue

Heart Channel

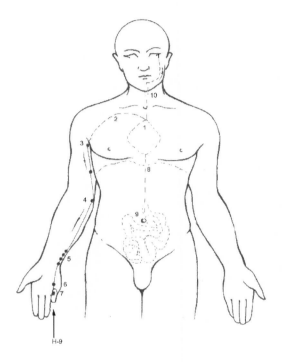

H-9

Small Intestine Channel –The function of the Small Intestine is to receive food, aid in digestion, and absorbs water and nutrients.

Small Intestine Channel

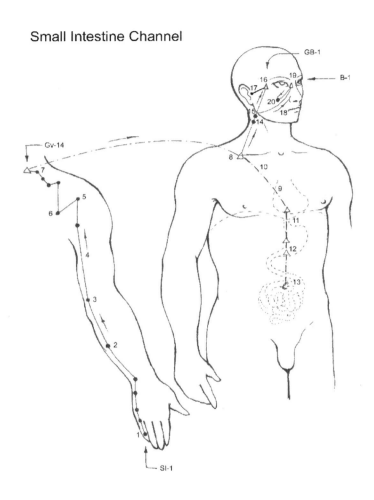

Urinary Bladder Channel - Stores and releases urine

Urinary Bladder Channel

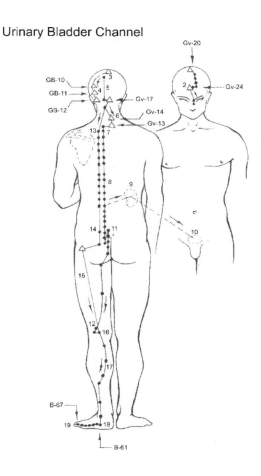

Kidney Channel – The Kidney stores *Jing* (Essence) and governs growth and maturation and reproduction, dominates water metabolism, assists in gathering of Qi from the Lungs, dominates the bone, builds marrow, and brain, manifests in hair, opens into the ears, controls the orfices of urination and bowel movement

Kidney Channel

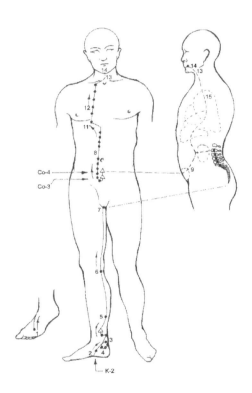

Pericardium Channel - In Chinese Medicine, the Pericardium protects the Heart

Pericardium Channel

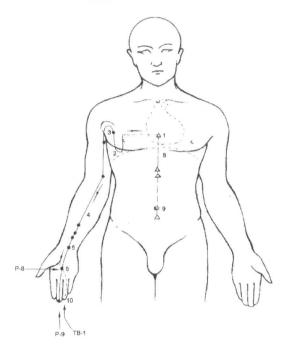

San Jiao Channel – With no equivalent in Western Medicine, the *San Jiao* acts as a passageway for Qi and its functions, assists all the other organs in their functions

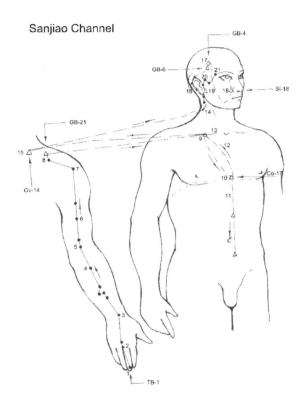

Sanjiao Channel

Gall Bladder Channel – The Gall Bladder stores and excretes bile, and governs decision making.

Gallbladder Channel

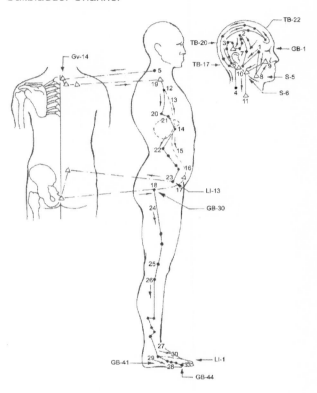

Liver Channel – The Liver stores and purifies blood, maintains the free flow of Qi in the body, controls the tendons and the nails. The Liver also opens into the eyes.

Liver Channel

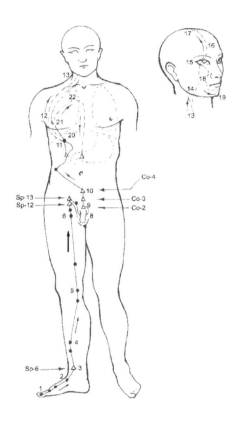

This is the critical rule for the proper qigong and internal arts practice. When synchronized with breathing, the Yin flow is synchronized with exhaling, and Yang flow is synchronized with inhaling. Furthermore, the body movement, breathing, and Qi flow are synchronized together. And finally, the *Jin* or force flow is further synchronized with the movement, breathing, and qi flow direction.

Using the *Biu Jee* finger strike of Wing Chun Kuen as an example, when one extends the arm outward at exhale, the Qi flows from the chest to the fingers along the arm three yin channels, while the force flow is transported from chest to the fingers. Thus, an efficient balance and properly designed qigong or martial arts form (set) is designed in this way. In addition, due to the consideration of the speed of the Qi flow and blood flow (Chinese Medicine blood concept) a properly designed set will start the left movement and followed by the right movement. This is why in the forms on Wing Chun Kuen that they start on the left side and follow on the right side.

In addition to the twelve regular channels, there are Eight Extraordinary Channels which are not directly linked to the major organ system, but have various functions such as the following:

a, they act as reservoirs of Qi for the twelve regular channels, filling and emptying as required;

b, they help circulate the Qi over the trunk of the body and, as such, play an important role in maintaining of good health;

c, they provide connections between the twelve regular channels.

It is a must for practitioners of the Chinese Internal Martial Arts to know how and where to access the qi energy of the body to facilitate the healing and strengthening process. On the other hand, the Channel system is also the basis of blocking Qi flow, or damaging Qi Flow, such as the pressure point strikes.

In order for Qi to flow smoothly according to the channel, the physical body needs to be in a loose state, mind in a quiet state, and the breathing in the natural low abdominal effortless Breathing State. This is the first state of the Energy element, or the Qi ready state. Unless this state is accomplished, qi flow will not flow upward, downward, in and out, smoothly. Thus, it is not likely to jump right away into practicing Qi manipulation without accomplishing the Qi ready state.

The second state of the Qi Element is the State of Qi surfaces naturally. In this State, the Physical Body Element, the Mind Element, and the Breathing Element are refined beyond the Qi Ready State. Qi flow will surface naturally without any artificial manipulation when the energy is filled up, similar to a charged battery. At this State, one might feel light weight, warm, or different sensations depending on the condition of the practitioner's body. As an example, the 1840's era *Siu Lin Tau* states, "Union in the *Dan Tian*, the Du channel sinks" (會合丹田督脈降), this describes the Qi Surfaces State.

The third State of the Qi Element is the State of one directing the Qi flow with one's intention or visualization, or the "Mind Directing Qi State". Here, one can direct the Qi to flow along the channel naturally to remove blockages, or strengthen the body, or internal organs, if one desires, or one just lets the Qi to flow by itself naturally. This Mind Directing Qi State is the State, as mentioned in the 1840's Red boat era *Siu Lin Tau* writing as, "Spiral twisting naturally, follow the breathing and the direction of the Qi channel" (旋迴自然順脈氣).

However, one must know that Qi development is never a "one size fits all" practice. One needs to practice based on one's body condition and constitution. For example, for those who have Yang Deficiency, it is only suitable to practice the "Qi Transportation method", and those who have Yin deficiency, it is suitable to practice the "Relaxation Method".

In terms of paying attention to specific area practice, those who have high blood pressure should be aware of their Kidney 1 Bubbling Spring point. (Editor's note: Kidney 1, *Yong Quan* or "Bubbling Spring" is found on the sole of the foot, in the depression while in plantar flexion, approximately at the anterior third and the posterior two thirds of the line from the web between the 2nd and 3rd toes to the back of the heel. It is used lower blood pressure, and treats headaches in acupuncture practice.) Those who have low blood pressure will get into trouble if focusing awareness to the Kidney 1 Bubbling Spring point. Those who have Kidney Yin Deficiency should not practice being aware of the lower *Dan Tian* because being aware of *Dan Tian* will raise the fire and cause the Kidney Yin to further be deficient.

Focus on *Dan Tian* will cause Qi stagnation in lower abdomen. Focus on the Yin Tang point will cause Qi flow to stagnate in head and interrupt the natural Qi flowing downward. Strong breathing, or intense intention, will cause strong fire to burning or draining of the Qi (壮火食气) . In terms of leading Qi flow practice, the Qi flow must raise from Kidney 1 Bubbling Spring point upward, instead of Qi flowing down from *Dan Tian* to Kidney 1 Bubbling Spring point which drains the Kidney Qi.

Thus, unless one has an experienced and trained teacher, it is better to not touch the Qi training to avoid endangering oneself, be it in Qigong, healing arts, or martial arts. As the first System key addresses, practice must be accord to the law of physics, law of natural human body, and traditional Chinese medicine theory and practice. Violation of these is looking for trouble. In the 1950's, there even were reports that the increase or add in complexity practice of some *Tai Ji Quan* sets in China caused imbalances that might lead to stroke or other health problems, due to the original design of the set is martial art based and violates the traditional Chinese Medicine Qi handling theory and practice.

In addition, a balance complete Qi element practice, be it in qigong, internal martial arts, or healing arts, must consist of two parts: The "Training of Qi" (練氣) and "Growing of Qi" (養气).

The Training of Qi part is for improving circulation, balancing, and/or removing blockages or stagnation. This is a dissipative practice.

The Growing of Qi part is for letting the body naturally cultivate the Qi. This is a charging or accumulative Qi practice.

Both parts are needed. Missing the Growing of Qi part will cause the Qi to be drained. Missing the Training of Qi part will not improve Qi flow circulation. As an example, it is common for a holistic practice to stand still to Grow the Qi, after a practice of a fist set, to Train the Qi.

Imbalance

Imbalance 偏差, is common in the practice of qigong, internal martial arts, healing qigong, or spiritual meditation. The root cause of the imbalance is mainly from:

a, jumping right into the mind leading Qi state practice without have the accomplishment of the prerequisite state in the physical body, mind, breathing, and Qi element, and
b, have no proper understanding on the Qi channel theory and practice.

This type of improper practice will cause overly intense handling, unknown blockages, self-generated tension, and or misdirecting the Qi flow. Even worse, the practitioner takes the sensations caused by the malpractice, imbalance, blockage, or stagnation to be a sign of achievement, and have the practitioner chase for these sensations. A common sensation, which is misleading, is heat or warmth in the body. Heat or warmth in an area, or flow in the body, is not an indication of proper practice. In fact, heavy breathing and heavy intention can cause warm to hot sensations in the body. It is critical to stop these practices immediately and to have an experienced qigong expert to coach and correct the imbalances, as failing to do so will result in many health or mental problems.

Finally, It is better to not work with the Qi Element without an experienced teacher. By evidence, not all qigong is legitimate, nor can all claims be delivered, be it an internal martial art, qigong, or spiritual meditation practice. One must look to find out the track record of the Qi practice one considers to practice seriously, before one practices it. Claims, one should not trust, one must check out the track record, find out its benefit, including its side effects. Working with Qi Element is similar to working with herbal prescriptions, as one shouldn't take any herbals or drugs, before one knows the benefits and risks of the medication. And, in general, working with the Physical Body Element, Mind Element, and Breathing Element in the directions of loose, quiet, and natural to indirectly develop the Qi Element is always a safer solution.

Chapter 6
Strength

Forward and reverse complement each other within the applications.

---- *Emei 12 Zhuang*

Jin 劲 in Chinese means a lively use of *Li* strength 力 or force. In a physics sense, this lively use of strength is a time dependent resultant force vector which is derived or moving, or "flows" from one end to the other through the physical body. The term "force flow" is coined from this "flowing" phenomenon. Force flow can be a time dependent linear or spiral flow. Force flow moves along a force flow path. Force flow can be analogous to water in a pipe. Water flows from one end to the other end of a pipe, dependent on time. The water pipe would be the force flow path. Thus, the handling of *Jin,* or force flow, relies on the timely activation and sequencing of the physical body's tendons and joints. This is different than the common handling of strength where one mainly tenses and loosens the physical body.

All Ancient Chinese Arts consist of *Ti* 体 body of the art, and *Yong* 用, the application of the art. The first four of the Six Core Elements are the *Ti* body of the art, and the last 2 elements, the Strength Element and Force Flow Element, are the *Yong* application, of the art. Without proper development of the first four elements, it will be difficult to fully develop the last two elements.

Preoccupied with self-generated tension, forcing, breath stagnation, and momentum are areas that the common practitioner is usually unaware of, and they need to be continually refined or improved for those who have learned the Six Core Elements. The continuous refinement or improvement is the bottom line of *gung fu* cultivation. It is through this continuous improvement or refinement, that the handling of force flow becomes more and more efficient and effective.

In order to handle strength, one needs to know the following phenomenon: power generation, coupling with the ground, action and reaction forces, body type and force flow type of power handling, physical body trajectory, force flow path and force flow, force flow injection, and linear and rotational (torque) types of force handling.

There are two basic types of power generation: 1) from your opponent; and 2) self-generated power. Power from your opponent is a way to borrow from your opponent's strength. For example, if he pushes you, you make borrow his incoming force.

As for self-generated power, generally, there are two types of self-generated power: 1) Power generated by muscle and tendons, and 2) Power generated by gravity, due to one's weight. For example, lying down on bed, body weight, and gravity are the sources of power generation. One can generate a lot of power effectively by manipulating the physical body weight and gravity. These two are the most basic power generations, and one can certainly fuse these two types of power generation to suit one's application.

Coupling with the ground, refers to one transfers or delivers force back and forth to other people or to the ground. One can observe and experience coupling in the following ways:

1) By pushing into a sponge which is placed on a wall with your palm, and observe how the applied force is delivered into the wall,

and received back into your palm; (i.e. Newton's action and reaction force).

2) Place a sponge under your feet to see, observe, and be aware how your force couples from your feet into the ground through the sponge, and is received back to your feet.

Figure above: Coupling

Every time one applies force, there will be a reaction force. We can observe the action and reaction forces using our palm to push into a washing sponge. As the sponge is pressed and pushed into the wall via the sponge, one feels the reaction force "reflect" back from the wall.

Figure above: Action and reaction force

The common or default strength handling method is what I refer to as the Body type power handling. In this type of handling, one uses the strength or force generated to first move the limb in order to crush the target. This is body type of power handling. One uses the body as a medium to deliver power to the target. An example would be hammering a nail. One grasps the hammer and swings it to hit the nail.

Also, the daily common acts of tensing up, holding, sustaining, or withstanding the body, are examples of body type of power handling. An example is pushing a car, in which you would need body type of power handling. In this type of power handling, the body is like a rod, and with all the joints locked up, and one uses the body to hold up, support, withstand or sustain the car while pushing it.

In addition, punching is done by using the force one generates to move one's arm and fist, and then hit the object or target with the trajectory of the fist.

Figures above - The trajectory of the fist and reaction force generated at the target.

From the body type handling examples above, one only focuses on action force, and has no concern with reaction force. Thus, reaction force one generates while creating the action force is usually countered by another self-generated action force. One does not made use of the reaction force. Instead, one generates another action force to counter the reaction force. Thus, this way of power handling or handling of strength is not efficient, but highly dissipative.

On the other hand, *Jin* or Force flow handling, is the type of handling where one uses the strength or force generated to press into the target directly with very minimal body movement. The force delivery has a specific direction, acting time, and sequencing. Due to it being a force directly applied to the target, it is implementing the force low. The specific direction, acting time, and sequencing is the reason it was named force flow.

It is different when compared to body type of handling, where one moves the body and has a trajectory of the body. Force flow handling uses the force flow path to deliver the power. As an example, while pressing into a wall with palm, wrist, elbow, and shoulder, these parts are all loose, and one will sense the reaction force from the wall travel back toward the palm, wrist, elbow, and shoulder. The path of the reaction force that travels from the palm to the shoulder is the force flow path. The trajectory which travels from the palm to the shoulder is the force flow.

Figure above: Force flow path of the reaction force flow travel up the arm.

As soon as any joint between the palm to the shoulder, let's say for example, the wrist, is tensed or held tightly or locked up, the reaction force force flow path is broken and reaction force force flow will be interrupted at the locked wrist joint. Thusly, body type of power handling is different, as force flow handling needs to be done in a loose physical state.

The body type of power handling uses tense physical body and deals with trajectory, while the force flow type directly uses the force flow via the flow path. Moving the physical body takes more time and is slower, while injecting of force flow with minimum physical movement is faster in comparison because the body doesn't have to move much.

There are two types of force flow injection and these are 1) the action force injection, and 2) the reaction force injection. An example for the action force injection is: when one presses one's palm into a wall with one's physical body in a loose state, one is injecting an action force into the wall, and at the same instant, the reaction force generated from this action force injection travels from the wall towards the body, via the force flow path, from the palm towards the shoulder. In addition, one also uses the intention to lead the force flow injection to travel into different depths.

An example of reaction force injection is: to make use of the force from the opponent pressing into one as an action force, leading this force to ground, to generate a reaction force, and then directing this reaction force to inject back to the opponent. This all happens instantaneously. Or, we may borrow the opponent's incoming force as an action force, convert it into a reaction force, then use this reaction force to inject back to the opponent.

The ability to handle force flow allows one when encountering an opponent skilled in force flow power handling, to sense and track them, so one knows how to handle an opponent skilled in this. Thus, one senses or "listens" to the strength to find out if the opponent is a body type strength or a force flow type strength and deal with it accordingly. Advanced players of strength are those who can effectively handle both the body type and force flow type power as if playing.

Finally, there are linear types, and rotational (torque) types of force handling. A linear type of force handling is again, similar to pushing a car where a force vector is in a linear manner. A rotational type of force handling is akin to a wrench and nut or bolt torque handling.

Figure on next page: Torque type of force handling. Close body power handling with rotational or torque and its advantage in close range play

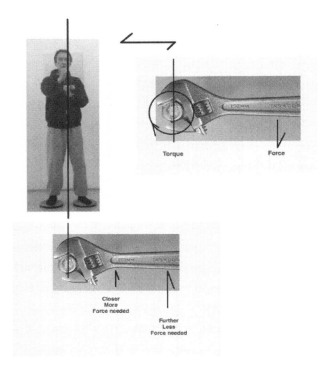

In general, close body force handling are rotational or torque types of force handling, similar torqueing a nut with the incoming force. However, one must condition and develop one's body in order to handle rotational or torque type of force handling.

Figure - Linear type of force handling

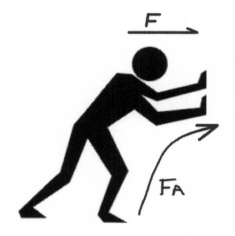

Figure: Linear and spiral force flow

Figure above: Using intention to lead the force flow injection depth

In order to handle the force flow operation effectively, one needs to develop the seven bows as in the figure. The seven bows are seven parts of the body. They include the feet, ankle, knee, hip (hip joints and lower part of spine), shoulder (shoulder and shoulder blade), elbow and wrist. Thus, the development of the first four elements is critical. Only with a proper body of the art is developed, can one have an alive and agile seven bows. For example, a closed physical element will cause a locked hip bow, unable to have proper lower abdominal breathing, causing stagnation in Qi flow, and a breakdown in the force flow path.

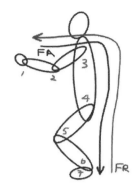

Figure above: Reaction force injection with seven bows

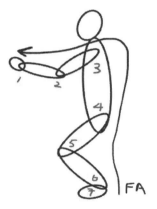

Figure above: Action force injection with seven bows

70

Chapter 7

Momentum

Do not be against the rushing horse's forward thrust,
laterally lock up the wild buffalo's feet

----- *Emei 12 Zhuang*

If an object is in motion, then it has momentum. Momentum can
be defined as "mass in motion." It is a physics term. According to
the physics, momentum is the product of mass and velocity, or
Momentum = Mass x Velocity. Since this is a physical world, all
physical action is subject to momentum. Combat is a physical
action. Therefore, the game of combat is based on the
manipulation of momentum.

Momentum or *Shi* 勢 is the core of combat, according to the
ancient Chinese, referring to both creating momentum and making
use of momentum. The term, "momentum play", is well illustrated
in the Chapter Five of *Sun Tzu's Art of War*.

"The rush of torrential waters tossing boulders illustrates momentum. The strike
of a bird of prey breaking the body of its target illustrates timing. Therefore, the
momentum of those skilled in warfare is overwhelming and their timing precise.
Their momentum is like a drawn crossbow and their timing is like the release of
the trigger. Therefore, those skilled in moving the enemy use formation that
makes the enemy respond. They offer bait that which the enemy must take,
manipulating the enemy to move while they wait in ambush.

One who exploits momentum commands men into battle like rolling logs and boulders. Logs and boulders are still when on flat ground, but roll when on steep ground. Square shapes are still, but round shapes roll. Therefore, those skilled in warfare use force by making the troops in battle like boulders rolling down a steep mountain. This is momentum."

Different Ancient Chinese martial arts have their uniqueness of playing the momentum game.

The following are some examples:

The famous *Wing Chun Maxims* of fighting ---- "Retain what comes in, Follow what retreats; Rush in on loss of contact", is a momentum play, while techniques are just an implementation of it. The key is the momentum handling, while there are implementations based on different conditions.

From the *Taijiquan* classic - "There are many boxing arts, although they use different types of momentum, for the most part they don't go beyond, the strong dominating the weak, and the slow resigning to the swift. The strong defeating the weak, and the slow hands ceding to the swift hands are all the results of natural abilities, and not of well-trained techniques. From the sentence, "A force of four ounces deflects a thousand pounds", we know that the technique is not accomplished with brute force."

Basically there are two types of momentum. These are 1) **Simple Momentum**, for example, a single punch or attack, and 2) **Complex Momentum**, for example, a combination attack or tactical set up move sequence.

Within Simple Momentum, there are **sharp strikes** and **power strikes**. The snapping or sharp strike, for example, a sun fist or vertical fist snapping strike, is more effective against a flexible target. The snapping action is an impulse which creates the velocity for high impact without pushing the target object. The power strike, or high momentum strike, for example, would be a straight middle punch used to move the target object.

The physics of collisions are governed by the laws of momentum.

Mathematically,

$F = m \bullet a$ (F = Force, m = mass, a = change in velocity / time),

or $F = m \bullet \Delta v / t$

And, Impulse = Change in momentum = $F \bullet t = m \bullet \Delta v$

And, Momentum = mass x velocity

Long fists and short strikes
Ancient martial arts can be generalized into two stereotypical range types: they are the Long Fist or *Chang Quan* 長拳 and the Short Strike or *Duan Da* 短打.

The concept of long fist is that both parties keep a distance of about two feet for counter attack. The play is to dynamically keep this two foot distance with footwork to counter attack with the goal of out striking the opponent. The body type of long fist is, in general, a bracing or withstanding type in which both parties tend to push each other away. Southern Martial art systems such as Fujian White Crane, Choy Lee Fut, and Northern Long Fist belong to the Long Fist category. One can find many interesting body trajectories to facilitate and implement this form of momentum play.

Figure below: Long range with the required distance, notice that the shoulder is in front of the body

The concept of short strike is to get to a "shoulder touching chest" at close range. The goal is sticking, trapping, throwing, or striking the opponent. The body type of the short strike is similar to "hugging each other", instead of the "withstanding body type" of the long fist art which engages in pushing each other away. Due to the limited narrow space the close body type is working in, an expert in close body short strike art is using the force flow path for force flow play. They do not engage in the long fist body trajectory long arm momentum play. Furthermore, due to the differences in characteristics of these two types of art, their entering and closing gap footwork are also different. Ancient Wing Chun Kuen, and Shaolin *Duan Da Quan* are good examples of the short strike art. Instead of letting the incoming force towards the central axis to move the physical body, one converts the incoming action force into torque through rotation, and delivers the reaction force of the incoming action force, back into the source of the incoming force.

Figure below: Close body range, where shoulder is not in front of the body

Body entering, or *Ru Shen* 入身, shows the uniqueness of the short strike. It has a different strategy compared with the long fist which is supported by the position, body work, footwork, and timing.

Short fist entering body is similar to a "snake coiling up a stick", where a snake climbs up the stick that is used to beat it, to attack the stick holder. The snake takes away the space between himself and the snake beater, to leave the beater no room to attack again.

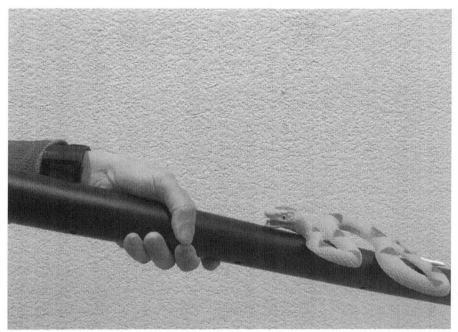

Figure above: The snake coils up the stick

In the Chapter Five of *Sun Tzu*, there is a passage, "There are not more than five musical notes, yet the combinations of these five give rise to more melodies than can ever be heard." The following are the five ways of handling momentum:

1, Give birth, or *Sheng* 生, to make use of incoming momentum. This is to make use or borrow the incoming momentum to power a desired momentum. For example, using the opponent's push to power a turning kick.

2, Subduing, or *Ke* 克, to counter against. This is to withstand the incoming momentum, such as blocking a punch.

3, Controlling, or *Zhi* 制. This is to control the incoming momentum; for example, control the central axis of the opponent by pressing into the elbow of the opponent, which results in controlling the opponent's momentum.

4, Dissolving, or *Hua* 化. This is to receive the incoming momentum; similar to receiving an incoming basketball passed to you.

5, The power of weight, or *Yong Su* 用数. This is to take advantage of the relatively larger momentum, such as a bigger, heavier weight person using the advantage of his mass. Or a smaller, lighter person taking advantage of his agility to create a huge impulse, or change of momentum.

Furthermore, these five basic ways of handling momentum have all kinds of different combinations for the momentum play. For example, receiving an incoming punch strike, and converting it for one's advantage to control the opponent. In this type of play, it will involve circular motion manipulation, which converts the incoming linear momentum into an angular or rotational momentum.

There are two common momentum practices in combat, and these are: 1) "Single Momentum subdues ten techniques", *Yi li jiang shi hui* 一力降十会 – This means one relies on a high speed, and/or heavy momentum to slip in, to crash, and/or overpower any techniques one faces; 2) using "soft to defeat hard", *yi rou ke gang* 以柔克刚。 This means one makes use of the five ways of momentum handling to elegantly handle the incoming attack.

In general, there are five basic types of entering momentum for combat. These are needed to cover the basics in momentum play. And these five momentum types have a different position, footwork, bodywork, and timing to support each of them.

The following are the five types of entry momentum for combat:

1) Direct entry - This is to directly attack the opponent center axis face to face.

2) Side entry - This is to attack the opponent central axis from side.

3) Step off return entry - This is to counter attack the opponent's central axis when one is trapped from the side, by stepping off the line of fire and returning.

4) Forward turn return entry - This is to counter attack the opponent's central axis when one is attacked from the back, by forward turning and returning.

5) Backwards turn return entry - This is to counter attack the opponent's central axis when one is attacked from the back, by backwards turning and returning.

Figure below: Direct entry

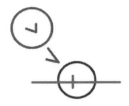

Figure above: Side entry

Figure above: Step off return entry

Figure below: Forward turn return entry

Another key element in the momentum play is the "momentum depth" resulting from a high momentum strike. "Momentum depth" is defined as the depth the incoming high momentum strike can penetrate. For example, a heavy truck colliding into a wall has deeper penetration than a light small car. In combat, one might needs to step aside with one step backward to receive a deep penetration momentum, since stepping aside alone might still not be adequate to dissolve the incoming strike.

To handle momentum effectively and efficiently, knowing Newton's Laws of Motion are a must. Newton's Laws of Motion state three concepts:

1, An object won't move by itself, and once in motion, it won't stop unless some force acts upon it.

2, The rate of change of momentum is directly related to the force acted upon it. In other words, when an object is pushed with more force, it will move faster and further away.

And 3, To every action, there is equal and opposite reaction.

Figure above: Backward turn return enter

To observe the natural of momentum handling in the real life

First, observe what happens when one walks in a straight line from a stationary position. Initially it takes more energy to start the movement, and as one picks up speed it requires less energy to sustain the movement. This observation shows Newton's concept of an object won't move by itself, and once in motion, it won't stop unless some force acts upon it. From this observation, one can experience the timing and energy needed in order to effectively handle momentum.

Second, observe what happens when while walking in a straight line and then radically change directions 90 degrees to the left or right. One will experience that a lot of energy is needed to make the change. The body's momentum wants to continue forward, so one needs to decelerate before one can make a turn to the new direction. From this simple change of direction in the walking experiment, one finds that natural footwork, timing, deceleration, and position handling is very important here. Without proper handling, one will cause instability, waste of energy, time delay, or counter-productive action. This observation further shows the above three Newton's laws of motion. Multiple variables are present in these two simple walking and turning experiments. By assessing and experiencing the variations, one is able to anticipate how the body will behave and predict the outcomes. These are how positioning, timing, footwork, and energy are designed and need to be handled in combat.

In addition, the understanding of the center of gravity, is also a must, in handling momentum in combat, which is dynamic. Every object has a center of gravity. Every person has a center of gravity as well. Simply put, the center of gravity is a determining factor in balance. If the center of gravity is in balance, then so is the object. However, if the center of gravity is thrown off balance, then the object will either be supported or will topple! When a force is applied directly on the center of gravity of a free object, the object will move directly in the direction of the force with the appropriate acceleration. When a force away is applied from the center of mass, the object will rotate around the center of gravity; thus, these are also basic to the momentum game.

Furthermore, the understanding of the vertical line of gravity, which is a vertical line which passes through center of gravity is critical for handling momentum in combat; the vertical line is also named as the centerline or central axis. An attack to this line will cause the opponent's static structure or dynamic momentum stability and trajectory to be disrupted. At contact range, to disrupt or control of this vertical line of gravity is usually done through manipulation of the neck, elbow, and legs. At noncontact range, disrupt or control of the vertical line of gravity can be done tactically by baiting the opponent to switch positions, thus creating an open or position and timing for entry.

Dealing with an opponent with the same technical skills or who knows the same techniques.

In this example, we use a 220 lb (100 Kg) person and a 154 lb (70 Kg) person.

The momentum the 100 Kg person generates a 1m/s speed is 100 Kg x 1m/s = 100 U

This means the energy produced or needed is (m x V sq.)/2 = (100 x 1)/2 = 50 U

In order for the 70 Kg person to produce equal amount of momentum, it requires them to increase their velocity to 1.42 m/s.

This means the energy produce or needed is (m x V sq.)/2 = (70 x sq. 1.42)/2 = 71.42 U

This means the 70 Kg person has to produce a 71.42 U energy which is 71.42/50 = 1.43 times or 43% more energy than the 100 Kg person.

Thus, the smaller person is at a disadvantage because with every move, he has to use 42% more energy just to be on par.

In order to compensate for this disadvantage, the smaller person needs an engine which is more efficient than the heavier person, this is where the development of the body of the art, (the "engine") is needed for the lighter weight or smaller person.

85

Thus, a lighter person with the same type of engine similar to the heavier person is always at a disadvantage even if they have the same level of momentum handling skill. Thus, the poor mechanics of the Post-1950's Wing Chun Kuen, which is missing the body of the art development, simply doesn't work well in this case.

Thus, the 6 13 3 process is needed. That gives more alternatives and degrees of freedom. Having 6 13 3, however, doesn't guarantee a win, but at least a chance to be on par.

In conclusion, one needs to know both the Strength Element and Momentum Element to play in the combat game. Footwork, body work, timing, positioning, and techniques are the variable components for realizing or implementing the momentum and the strength one needs to get the job done. In Wing Chun Kuen, the Chi Sau practice and wooden dummy set practice are tools of studying and mastering the Wing Chun Kuen way of momentum and strength play.

Chapter 8

A Balance

Compassion is within the Asuras' heart,
the disciples of the Buddha take the precept of not killing or hurting
living beings.

----- *Emei 12 Zhuang*

General types of Chinese Martial Arts

Chinese martial arts can be categorized into two different types: the
hard, abrupt, and intense type, and the soft, balanced, and gradual
type.

Explosive, fast, hard, intense types of martial arts is suitable for the
young and healthy, however, it is not suitable for those who are
older than 40 years old.   It is known in China martial art track
records that this type of martial art practice is very likely to cause
internal organs damage or illness.   The soft, balanced, and gradual
type martial art on the other hand are suitable for those who are
older than their 40's, or having a weaker health.   This type of
martial arts support good health and are able to improve mind and
body.

Even though soft, balanced, and gradual type martial art is suitable
for those over 40, any martial arts practice needs to be within
suitable duration to avoid over practice. There is a general rule of
thumb that can help one to determine the limitation of one's
martial art practice. And that is, to monitor one's heart beat such
that it does not exceed one's limit based on one's age.

For Males:

Maximum heart beat per minute = $209 - (0.69 \times Age)$

Suitable martial arts practice heart beat per minute not to exceed = Maximum heart beat x 0.7

For Females:

Maximum heart beat per minute = $205 - (0.75 \times Age)$

Suitable martial arts practice heart beat per minute not to exceed = Maximum heart beat x 0.7

In general, most of those who are aged from 20 years old to 79 years old, the soft, balanced, and gradual type of martial arts practice of 30 to 60 minutes daily could improve one's health or physical condition. It is best to consult one's health care provider or family doctor for advice on one's martial art practice, since every individual is different.

In addition, it is a common practice that one avoids: training under extreme temperatures or training in a windy area. All practice must be gradual, instead of abrupt and shocking, which causes the body to be imbalanced or injured. Intake of cold beverages right after training or with meals also cause imbalance and are draining on one's energy. It is a rule of the thumb that after sexual activity, one must take a rest, up to four hours, before one can practice internal arts, in order to avoid strain, or severe discharge of energy. Also, only practice internal arts one hour before or after meals.

Following the Five Precepts is a Buddhist martial art tradition, which exists in the ancient writing of Shaolin martial art or *Emei 12 Zhuang*. The purpose of taking precepts is to guard or protect one from misbehaving or misusing one's martial arts. That is to develop a habit of not getting into gray areas, which might lead one to violate a moral code, or violation of law. The Five Precepts are:

1) not killing, 2) not stealing, 3) not engaging in sexual misconduct, 4) not lying, and 5) not consuming intoxicants

"The Buddha told Ananda, "You constantly hear me explain in the *Vinaya* that there are three unalterable aspects to cultivation. That is, collecting one's thoughts constitutes the precepts; from the precepts comes *Samadhi*; and out of *Samadhi* arises wisdom. *Samadhi* arises from precepts, and wisdom is revealed out of *Samadhi*. Your basic purpose in cultivating *Samadhi* is to transcend the wearisome defilements. But if you do not renounce your thoughts of killing, you will not be able to get out of the suffering. "

---- Shurangama Sutra

Appendix – The Yik Kam Siu Lin Tau Kuen Kuit

中华文化遗产，祖宗之教，故不敢遗弃，亦不敢加以篡改。不願不敢为中华历史罪人也。

The heritage of traditional Chinese culture, the teaching of our ancestors, I dare not to abandon it, or dare not to tamper with it. I am unwilling to and dare not to change it, because I do not want to become a sinner in traditional Chinese history.

今不敢私藏，盡所知，所能，如实和盤托出公于天下，只求為後人盡棉薄之力。缺陷之處，不週之處，猶请諸大德見諒。

I dare not selfishly keep this for myself. Here, I present all as I know as it is, and I hope to help the future generations with my very insignificant effort. If there is error or imperfection, I beg for your pardon.

太平天國年代红船戲班中易金系小練頭視頻与歌訣全集。易金系小练頭共有四段，此為第一至四段視頻配合歌訣。拳釋訣，訣引拳。拳訣不二。

The Siu Lin Tau passed by Yik Kam in the Taiping Heavenly Kingdom Red Boat era is presented in the original writing and video. There are four parts to it. The writing describes the set. The set presents the writing. Set and writing are non-dual.

此套路之傳承：
易金是李文茂红船時代戲班正旦，在廣東番禺曹家傳授詠春拳，傳授此小練頭，易金祖師傳于曹順，曹順傳曹德勝，曹德勝傳曹全與曹安，先師公曹安傳先師曹雄才。

The transmission of this SLT set:
Yik Kam was an opera actor who play female role in the Lee Man Mau Red Boat era.
Yik Kam passed it to Cho Sun of Cho family in Poon Yee, Canton
Cho soon passed it to Cho Dak Shing
Cho Dak Shing passed to Cho Chin and Cho On.
My late Sigung, Cho On passed it to my late sifu, Cho Hong Choy.

Translation Version 1.4

易金詠春：小練頭歌訣
Yik Kam Wing Chun , Siu Lin Tau song kuit

斯是上乘法。通關開竅有奇功
This is an advanced method. Its wonderful result penetrates through the gates and attains realization.

若不明攻守之道、皆失過徧，弊耳。
If you are not clear with the concept of attack and defense (center line), you will be biased. That is a mistake.

Y Pre: (instruction prior to the details of the set)

Y Pre 1 眼要對手。
Eyes Must Track Hands.

Y Pre 2 手要對心。
Hands Must Track Heart.

Y Pre 3 手從心發。

Hand Issue from the Heart.

Y Pre 4 一絲不苟。
One Thread must not off.

Y Pre 5 一伸一縮。
Every Stretch, Every Contract.

Y Pre 6 柔中帶剛。
Within the soft there is hardness.

Y Pre 7 剛中而柔。
Within Hardness is Softness.

Note: the above expresses, for example, when the arm is fully extended and expands, it is referred as hard; and while the arm is contracting loosely, it is referred to as soft.

Y Pre 8 則是靜如平波, 動如翻江。
When the movement is slow it is analogous to a calm smooth wave
When the movement is large and fast, it is analogous to a huge violent wave (i.e. a Tsunami).

一 , Part 1

Y1 聚意會神平肩檔。
Focus the intention, union with the Shen, while in the equal shoulder stance

Y2 兩手前起分陰陽
Two Hands Front Raise Divide into Yin and Yang.

Y3 左腿踔出有善惡。
The trip out of the left leg has positive and negative effects.

Y4 右跟屈勁緊反藏
The bending power of the right heel tightly stores in the reverse direction.

Y5 會合丹田督脈降。
Union in the Dan Tian, Du channel sinks.

Y6 手臂鞭出橫力勁
The arm whips out the horizontal Jin

Y7 神寄指爪袖底旁。
Pay attention to the finger, claw, and the side under the sleeve.

Y8 旋迴自然順脈氣
Spiral twisting naturally, follow the breathing and the direction of the Qi.

Y9 掌背向外神意足。
Back of Palm Faces Outward, Intention is Full.

Y10 翻掌抽纏對心防
Rotating palm reeling guarding the heart.

Y11 單橫相撐合氣運。
Single horizontal and double press handling is in accord to breathing.

Y12 相抱沉身力橫分
Embracing and sinking, splits the force horizontally.

Y13 前虛急用擒伏法。
Forward Empty Urgently Use Seize Subdue methods.

Y14 下叉飛雙插翼忙
Lower intersection, flying double, Hurry piercing wings

Y15 合實雙掌穿心貫。
Joining the two palms, drive through the heart

Y16 下沉關元背攻上
Sinking down to Guan Yuan area, back of the palm attacks upwards.

Y17 一任自然脈安祥。
Following natural spontaneously, the qi will flow in a peaceful and balanced way.

Y18 企掌屈肘單昭陽
Erect palm bent elbow single zhao yang

Y19 上下飛花勁脈暢。
Upper and Lower Flying Flower Power Channels Smooth.

Y20 吞吐如虹發力罡
Swallowing and spitting are like a smooth rainbow issuing force.

Y21 下結關元參佛手。
Lower knot at *guan yuan* area (then turn into) Buddha counsel hands.

Y22 一任自然氣脈長
Following natural spontaneously the breathing, *zhen qi* and it flow will grow (strong)

二， Part 2

Ya1 手臂鞭出橫力勁。
Hand and arm whip out horizontal *Jin*.

Ya2 下旋往上企肘膀
Spiral downward then up turn into the vertical elbow wing.

Ya3 斜身舒腰劈豺狼。
Tilted the body expand the waist axe the jackal wolf

Ya4 膀肘拗腰流下訪
Wing elbow bending waist visit (the opponent) under the flow

Ya5 旋上鷹爪擒羊忙。
Spiral upward hurry capture the goat with eagle's claw

Ya6 袖底穿花五指插
Under sleeve penetrating flower five fingers thrust.

Ya7 回身中宮出手忙。
Return (re-capture) to the center door, the response must be in a hurry

Ya8 圈手擒拿左右撐
Circle hand, control and seize, left right palm strike

Ya9 挑橋奉印印胸膛。
Pick the bridge present the seal, sealing the chest.

Ya10 雙爪握拳脈氣爽
Double claws grasp fists the Qi meridians and breathing are comfortable

Ya11 雙掌下沉提氣上。
Sinking both palms, rise while inhaling

Ya12 拱手提氣吐無妨
Double push hands while exhaling

Ya13 雙掌翻出如壓頂。
Turn both palms and strike out similar to a mountain press down

Ya14 抽送往來如吐舌
Withdraw and send (the finger strike) similar to (snake) spits its tongue.

Ya15 雙掌互插分突圍。
Double palm thrusting each other to breakout sudden attack

Ya16 左右側腿勁如虹
Left and right kick support by smooth and powerful *Jin*

Ya17 右手鞭手橫中劈。
Right arm whip arm split horizontal to the center

Ya18 抽砍更需不誤遲
Draw and chop must be done without delay

Ya19 標指狠毒急可用。
Biu Jee is poison, use it at emergency

Ya20 回身中宮參佛手
Return (re-capture) to the center palace with Buddha hand.

三, Part 3

Yb1 敵強孤弱封喉手。
Enemy is strong while I am weak, using seal throat hand

Yb2 拱手折力要均勻
Double palms breaking the incoming force in an even way

Yb3 左外右肘偏身發。
Left and right elbow issue with slant body

Yb4 右肘企肘護心旁
Erect right elbow guard the heart area

Yb5 撕手能破長橋法。
Tearing hands is for breaking the long bridge.

Yb6 耕手上下有陰陽
Gang sau has yin yang within

Yb7 抽手鎖腿毒蛇舌。
Withdraw hand, lock leg, poison snake tongue

Yb8攞搥連環剛柔用
Stack punches chain strike in a hard and soft way

四，　Part 4

Yc1 左右耕手分陰陽。
Left and right gang sau consist of yin yang

Yc2 挑橋奉印上下分
Pick the bridge presents the seal with up and down split

Yc3 拱手用勁要平均。
Double palm power needs to be evenly applied

Yc4 圈手濺標連環吐
Circle hand splash spear chained spit

Yc5 左右撕手勁力均。
Left and right tearing hands with even *Jin*

Yc6 破碑胸肋致命喪
Broken monument target at chest ribs cause death

Yc7 虎手左右翻。
Tiger hand left and right flip

Yc8 攛搥準備用
Stack punch ready to use

Yc9 攤伏靜中藏。
Tan and Fuk hide within silence

Yc10 摽指上下左右用
Biu Jee uses in the up, down, left, and right direction

Yc11 抽鞭砍攛攻。
Withdraw, whip, chop, stack attack

Yc12 圈冚挑攛常要用
Circle outward, inward, pick, stack are often used

Yc13 劍指膀肘呈英雄
Sword finger bong elbow present to the hero

About the Author

Hendrik Santo, MScEE, is a power management semiconductor design architect based in the Silicon Valley California. He is a 40 year researcher of Wing Chun Kuen, and more than 20 years research in the Six Healing Sounds. He is also a grand student of Grandmaster Ma Li Tang of the Six Healing Sounds. He was a student of the Chan Patriarch, the late Venerable Master Hsuan Hua.

咏春 6.13.3

Made in United States
Orlando, FL
25 May 2022

18169664R00062